Creating
Angels

Creating Angels

STORIES OF
TZEDAKAH

retold by
Barbara Diamond Goldin

A

JASON ARONSON INC.
Northvale, New Jersey
London

This book was set in 12 pt. Berkeley Oldstyle

Copyright © 1996 Barbara Diamond Goldin

10 9 8 7 6 5 4 3 2 1

Library of Congress Cataloging-in-Publication Data

Goldin, Barbara Diamond.
    Creating angels : stories of tzedakah / retold by Barbara Diamond Goldin.
        p.   cm.
    Includes bibliographical references.
    ISBN 1-56821-531-2 (alk. paper)
    1. Charity.   2. Legends, Jewish.   3. Ethics, Jewish.   I. Title.
BJ1286.C5G65   1996
296.3'85—dc20   95-21161

Manufactured in the United States of America. Jason Aronson Inc. offers books and cassettes. For information and catalog write to Jason Aronson Inc., 230 Livingston Street, Northvale, New Jersey 07647.

For the staff and students of Heritage Academy, Longmeadow, Massachusetts—a place of learning, spirit, caring, and love

Contents

Contents

Acknowledgment

With gratitude to the Harold Grinspoon and Diane Troderman Tzedakah Fund, administered by the Jewish Endowment Foundation of the Jewish Federation of Greater Springfield, for the grant that helped support me in the writing of this book, and to Deborah K. Polivy, who helped me develop the idea for this grant.

Introduction

The twenty-four stories about *tzedakah* in this collection are from Jewish folklore and *midrash*, from Eastern Europe and countries like Tunisia and Afghanistan. Some are based on oral tales like "The Two Beggars," which is from Afghanistan, and "The Rabbi's Blessing" from Tunisia. Some stories like "A Town of Baruchs" and "The Rabbi and the Rag Dealer" are hasidic in origin, while others like "Ox and Herbs" and "The Two Keys" are from much older sources. All of the sources on which these retellings are based can be found in the books listed in the bibliography.

The Hebrew word *tzedakah* is often translated as charity. But it actually means something slightly different—it means justice or righteousness. According to our Sages, *tzedakah* means we have an obligation to give to those in need. We give not just when we feel the urge or if the mood strikes us. *Tzedakah* has always been such a key *mitzvah*, or commandment, for Jews throughout the centuries that the talmudic Sage Rabbi Assi said, "*Tzedakah* is as important as all the other commandments put together."

In Eastern Europe, before the Holocaust, families kept *pushkas*, *tzedakah* boxes, lined up on kitchen windowsills or above the stove. One *pushka* was for the land of Israel, another for the local burial society, another for the *yeshivah*, the school for the advanced learning of Torah, and so on. As a little girl visiting grandparents and great aunts and uncles in New York City, I can remember seeing these *pushkas* in their homes and taking them for granted.

Some people today are concerned that nothing is replacing these *pushkas* and that children do not have a concrete symbol of *tzedakah* around them daily. They are concerned with how to help children become aware of this crucial *mitzvah* and how important *tzedakah* is for the Jewish community as a whole.

One of these people, the author, lecturer, and poet Danny Siegel, has worked very hard to reintroduce this *mitzvah* to today's youth (and adults). He searches for *mitzvah* heroes in Israel and the United States and writes about them. He brings youth groups to meet them and collects money for their projects—projects such as providing wedding dresses for poor women, a home for abandoned Down's syndrome babies, and flowers for the elderly for *Shabbat*.

I have collected and retold these stories in the

hopes that perhaps they, too, will help us in our thinking about the *mitzvah* called *tzedakah*—help us in a time when most children no longer see a lineup of *pushkas* on the kitchen shelf or a *Shabbat* stranger invited for a meal.

I hope these stories will show that *tzedakah* is not just about giving money to the poor. It includes an attitude and encompasses a whole belief system. In the story "The Two Keys," we learn that our wealth is not our own but a gift from God to be used for the good of others as well as ourselves. And the story "The Evil Urge" shows how giving can transform the giver as much as it helps the receiver. In the Talmud it says that one who gives even the smallest coin to the poor is privileged to sense the presence of God.

Many of the people in these stories run to do a *mitzvah*. People like Yochanan in "The Watchman" or Rabbi Mordechai in "The Fragrance of Good Deeds" view it as a privilege to be able to give.

And, indeed, this is the way our Sages have viewed giving *tzedakah*. They say that even a poor person who himself takes from the *tzedakah* fund is obliged to give *tzedakah*. The *yeshivah* student Aryeh Lev does this in the story "The *Kaddish*." Everyone is obligated to give, and no one is to be shamed for being poor.

Our Sages said that a donor can even deceive a needy person who, because of pride, will not take money. The donor can allow him or her to think the *tzedakah* is a loan. There are examples of this in "The Rabbi and the Rag Dealer" and "The Loan." And we see to what great lengths Yonah the Water Carrier goes to prevent Moshe from being humiliated because of his sudden poverty.

There are also stories about how the Sages understood the psychology of being poor. In the Talmud, Shmuel, the son of Abba bar Ba, saw that a family who had taken *tzedakah* were eating expensive foods. When he told his father, Abba bar Ba said to give them more money, because the man was once rich and was now bitter about being poor. Let him adjust gradually. In these stories about *tzedakah*, we see dignity, honor, and respect instead of humiliation, shame, and embarrassment.

The Talmud is often very specific about the *mitzvah* of *tzedakah*. Giving between 10 and 20 percent of our income and gifts to *tzedakah* is recommended (Hello to those becoming *bar* or *bat mitzvah!*). Giving more than one-fifth of our income is not recommended because it may cause the giver to become poor.

The Sages say that we should take care of the needs of our immediate family first, then our relatives, then the larger community. Sometimes we see instances in talmudic and midrashic stories where pious Jews were so eager to give *tzedakah* that they gave away what was needed for their own families. This is true of the talmudic Sage Rabbi Elazar Ish Bartosa, who gave away his daughter's dowry to orphans. In these cases, *tzedakah* collectors tried to avoid, and even hide from, such overly generous givers so that these people would not give away what they themselves needed.

In his book *Mishneh Torah*, Maimonides outlined eight steps for giving *tzedakah*.

1. The highest form of *tzedakah* is aiding the poor to support themselves. This is what Rabbi Mordechai does in "The Fragrance of Good Deeds" and what Moshe and Rifka do in "The Town of Baruchs."

2. The second highest form is when neither the giver nor the receiver knows the identity of the other. This was the level of *tzedakah* carried out in a special chamber of the Temple in Jerusalem. Here people could leave money in secret, and the needy could take it in secret.

3. The third highest level is where the giver knows the receiver, but the receiver doesn't know the giver, as in the story "You Know What Friends Are For."

4. The fourth highest level is when the receiver knows the giver, but the giver does not know the receiver.

5. The fifth highest level is when the giver gives before being asked.

6. The sixth level is when the giver gives after being asked.

7. The seventh level is when the giver gives less than he or she should but does so cheerfully.

8. The eighth level is when the giver gives grudgingly.

Related to *tzedakah* is a category of *mitzvot* called *gemilut hasadim*, or acts of loving-kindness. *Tzedakah* is concerned with the giving of money and goods to the poor. Acts of loving-kindess, however, can be given to the rich as well as the poor, to the living as well as the dead, and they include the giver's time and energy as well as money. Some of the stories in this collection demonstrate *gemilut hasadim*. Aharon in "The Unusual Innkeeper" and Yochanan in "The Watchman" both offer hospitality to traveling merchants who are in need of help other than money. Thinking about and giving *tzedakah* lead us naturally to doing acts of loving-kindness as well.

By performing these *mitzvot, tzedakah,* and *gemilut hasadim*, we engage in *tikkun olam*, repair of the world. We experience the powerful feeling of doing good in our world, of creating angels. It is my hope that these stories will encourage young readers of today to create their own angels, even though they may never see a row of *pushkas* on a shelf in a little kitchen in Poland or on a windowsill in an apartment in the Bronx.

1
Mullah Avraham's Fine Silk Coat

ong ago in Persia, what is today called Iran, there lived a very learned and righteous man called Mullah Avraham. The title Mullah, meaning rabbi, was given him out of respect, though he was not actually a rabbi.

Although learned and righteous, Mullah Avraham was very poor. Whenever he was invited to a celebration, he would put some of the food into a bag to bring home. In this way, his family could also eat.

There was one thing that especially bothered Mullah Avraham about being poor. He was always given the most humble seat at celebrations. Sometimes, at first he would be seated closer to the table of honor where the bride or groom sat or the proud parents of a newborn baby. However, as wealthier or more important guests arrived, Mullah Avraham was expected to give them his seat. The waiters, of course, always served the people at the table of honor first, and then the people near them, and so on. By the time they reached Mullah Avraham at the back of the room or by the door, there would be practically nothing left on their serving trays—nothing but crumbs, that is.

I am seated at the back like a beggar, thought Mullah Avraham, as he looked about him at one fine wedding party. And there, in the front, are the men who can't read even one verse from the Torah and who do not treat their fellow human beings with any loving-kindness or decency. Is it because of the fine clothes they are wearing, then, that they are sitting in the front? It is certainly not because of their knowledge of Torah or their performance of *mitzvot*.

Then, one day, an old friend of his father stopped by Mullah Avraham's house. Mullah Avraham heard that this wealthy weaver, Yaacov, had sold his home and all that belonged to him so he could journey to the Holy Land. He wanted to spend his last years in David's city, Jerusalem.

"But I could not bear to sell this," Yaacov told Mullah Avraham as he held out a fancy silk dress coat. "My father gave it to me, and I wish you to have it in honor of all your good deeds and my friendship with your father."

Mullah Avraham was delighted with the present and wished Yaacov a safe journey.

The very next time Mullah Avraham was invited to a fancy celebration, he put on his new silk dress coat. When he entered the house, his host showed much surprise at Mullah Avraham's appearance. He looked grand indeed. This time, the host led Mullah Avraham to the table of honor. No crumbs or leftovers for Mullah Avraham now. He was served the finest of foods, the trays full, the meats, fish, and rice warm from the oven.

Mullah Avraham enjoyed the food and the wine, and when he was satisfied, he began to fill the pockets of his coat, first with handfuls of rice and meat stew, with vegetables, crisp and cooked, and then with sweets, nuts and candies and layered pastries all sticky with honey.

The other guests stopped their eating and stared at Mullah Avraham's odd behavior. Was he suddenly mad?

Mullah Avraham answered their stares by saying, "Without my coat, you sit me in the back of the room and feed me scraps. But with my fancy new coat, you sit me in the front with choice morsels. Therefore, it must be my fine coat you mean to feed and honor, and not me!"

2
The Water Carrier

osaf was a content man, and a good one. Each morning he woke up early, before his wife or seven children even stirred. He studied a page of Torah, said his morning prayers, and then walked to the riverbank, the long pole holding two pails balanced across his back. With a rhythm developed over years of working as a water-carrier, Yosaf filled the buckets, hoisted them on the pole, and carried them to customers, filling and carrying all day long. He was by no means wealthy from all this toil, but he and his family managed, and this was enough for Yosaf.

Then, and no one knew why, Yosaf changed. After working all day as a water carrier, he was seen begging in the evenings. From house to house Yosaf walked, palm out, asking for coins. Amazed whispers followed him.

"Scandalous that a man who can earn the money to support his family should beg too," the whisperers said.

"Trying to get rich at our expense," said others.

But they all gave just the same. One did not turn down a beggar.

One of the whisperers did go running to the rabbi, however. And a few days later, Yosaf was summoned to appear before the Sage.

"Do you make a living by being a water carrier?" inquired the rabbi.

"Thanks be to God, day by day," answered Yosaf. "We manage."

"Then why do you beg from door to door?"

Yosaf did not answer.

"I asked you a question," the rabbi said firmly.

Still no answer.

The rabbi grew impatient. "Since you earn enough from being a water carrier to support your family, you must promise me that you will stop your begging."

The only reply was silence.

"What is wrong with you, Yosaf? This is not like you." The rabbi stood up and leaned over the table toward Yosaf, his eyes bright with anger.

"I cannot promise," muttered Yosaf, lowering his eyes under the rabbi's stare.

It happened that the town's richest man, Shimon, was at that same moment sitting outside the rabbi's study, waiting to speak to the rabbi. He could hear what the rabbi said to Yosaf right through the closed door, the rabbi's voice was that loud.

Shimon's face grew red and his shoulders trembled.

He rushed into the rabbi's study and exclaimed, "It isn't what you think, Rabbi. This man is really a hidden saint."

Then he turned to Yosaf. "You must tell the rabbi what happened, my friend." And Shimon left, closing the door behind him.

The bewildered rabbi sat down. Yosaf, a hidden saint?

Yosaf cleared his throat. "I didn't want to tell anyone," he said. "It concerns Shimon. You know that each day I deliver water to those who can afford it. Shimon has always been one of my steady customers. But a few months ago, he stopped paying me.

"'I'll pay next week,' he would say. Next week would come and still no payment. But I kept bringing him water. He was always such a good customer.

"One day Shimon wasn't there and his wife, Rachel, answered the door. She pulled me aside. 'Shimon would never tell you,' she explained. 'He has too much pride. But our business failed and we have no money to pay our bills. That's why we haven't paid you. I don't know what we're going to do. Please, don't tell anyone what I've told you.'

"'I won't tell anyone,' I promised her.

"From that day on, I started begging. Of course, I never told anyone I was begging for Shimon. Let people talk about me. At least I could spare Shimon embarrassment and put some bread on his table until he got back on his feet. I hope you will forgive me for not answering your questions, Rabbi."

"Forgive you!" the rabbi jumped up from his chair and went over to embrace the water carrier.

"You do not need my forgiveness," he said. "How many people are there who would humble themselves to save another's pride as you have? I just pray to God that in the World to Come I will be fortunate enough to share a place beside you in Paradise."

3
Are Not the Ways of Heaven Wondrous?

endel had three daughters to marry off and no money for dowries.

My daughters will be forty years old and spinsters before I can save enough, he thought.

"Why not go to Mezhbizh and ask the Baal Shem Tov for some advice," suggested Golda, his wife. "Every day they grow older," she warned.

So Mendel traveled to see the great rabbi.

The Baal Shem greeted poor Mendel warmly and told him to travel to the town of Ger. "There, underneath the bridge, on the bank of the Vistula River, you will find a fortune—enough money to provide dowries for all your daughters."

It took Mendel several days to travel to Ger. But he found the bridge and, with his shovel, was about to begin digging in the riverbank when he heard a familiar voice call his name.

He looked up. Standing on the bridge was his old friend Simcha, a tailor now. He and Simcha had been boyhood friends in Kovle.

"What are you doing in Ger?" asked Simcha. "And with a shovel?"

So Mendel told Simcha his story about his three marriageable daughters. And their nonexistent dowries. And the Baal Shem Tov's instructions.

"And you really think you will find a treasure right here in the mud. Unlikely," said Simcha. "As unlikely as that dream I had just last night. Why, I dreamed I dug up a treasure under a big black kitchen stove with black-and-white tiles on its top on the street of the shoemakers in the town of Belz. Now, do you think I should go there and start digging too, my friend?" And after Simcha had had a few laughs, he looked down to his friend. But Mendel was nowhere to be seen.

Mendel, listening to Simcha, had recognized his very own stove and street and town in his friend's dream. He forgot all about digging by the river and hurried home to dig there.

By the time he reached his house, it was dark and late and his wife and daughters were asleep. Tired as he was, Mendel lit the lamp by the big black stove and began to dig in the dirt underneath.

It wasn't long before his shovel hit a hard object. He worked it loose from its age-old spot under the stove until he could dislodge what he found to be a small chest of silver and gold. His troubles, their troubles, were over.

The next day, Mendel sat Golda and his daughters down at the kitchen table, opened up the chest for all to see, and divided the treasure into four piles—three for dowries and a pile left over for a decent life for the parents too. Golda wasted no time in going to the matchmaker's, and soon they were all busy pinning and stitching wedding dresses for the soon-to-be brides.

There was an air of festivity and expectation in the little house, except Mendel wasn't feeling so festive. He was busy feeling guilty about his friend Simcha. For wasn't it due to Simcha's dream that he and his family were in such a good position?

So Mendel decided to return to Ger with some money to give Simcha—a tithe, that is, 10 percent of his fortune, to be exact.

He was halfway on the road to Ger when he heard his name called by that old familiar voice. There, around a bend in the road, came Simcha the tailor, who must have spotted Mendel first.

"Why, Simcha," said Mendel. "I was just on my way to see you."

"And I was on my way to see you," responded Simcha. "What a coincidence!

"You know, after you left, I got the strange idea in my head to dig where you were digging. Who knows where these ideas come from, *nuh*? I dug and dug, and just when I was thinking what a silly idea this all was, I struck something hard. Probably a rock, I thought. But I dug it out. A rock it wasn't. A chest of gold and silver coins it was. Amazing, no? My family and I have been living a lot better since that day, I'll tell you. But then I thought to myself, it isn't right. I must share this good fortune with my friend Mendel. If not for Mendel, I never would have found it. So here, I wrapped up 10 percent of my fortune for you."

Mendel was stunned and could not utter a word.

"You're not happy with 10 percent? Well then, I'll give you more—20 percent. Is that fair?"

"I don't believe this," muttered Mendel.

"Believe, believe," said Simcha.

"You don't know the half of it," said Mendel. "Here I was, sent by the Baal Shem Tov to dig for treasure under the bridge in Ger. But it appears that that treasure was destined for you. You send me to find a treasure in my very own kitchen. And at the exact moment that I decide to set out to find you to share my treasure, you set out to find me for the very same purpose. Are not the ways of Heaven wondrous?"

"Indeed," said Simcha, who, for once, was at a loss for words.

"The question now is what are we to do with this money we were going to give the other?" said Mendel. "It must be destined for some special purpose."

Simcha, regaining his wits, thought of an answer. "You said you have three daughters of marriageable age?"

"Yes," said Mendel. "The matches have not been decided upon yet. But soon."

"Well, I have a son of marriageable age," said Simcha. "Why don't we make a match of one of your daughters and my son and give this money to them?"

Mendel liked this idea of Simcha's. "Let's go together to Mezhbizh and tell the Baal Shem Tov what happened when I set out to follow his advice. Let's see what he says to our idea."

The two friends came to the Baal Shem. Before they even had a chance to open up their mouths, the rabbi's face lit up. "This is a match from Heaven," he said. "Both of you have been blessed, but you must make sure you use this wealth only for good. Treat this gift as money put into your trust for safekeeping, and you will continue to be blessed."

Simcha and Mendel stood there, gaping at the rabbi. How did he know? Was their story written all over their faces?

"And to begin with, a concrete act," said the Baal Shem. "You, Mendel, should provide a dowry for a poor orphan girl, while you, Simcha, do the same for a boy. Let these two marry a week before the celebration of your own children. And do not make the one celebration any less fine than the other. Then good fortune will surely follow you both."

And Mendel and Simcha did exactly as the rabbi instructed.

4
A Rich Woman's Diet

nce a wealthy woman named Malka came to Rabbi Dov Baer, the Maggid of Mezeritch, for his blessing.

The Maggid asked Malka, "And what do you eat at each meal?"

"Why I eat very sparingly and simply. Only bread and salt and water," said Malka proudly, thinking the Maggid would be pleased with her answer.

But the Maggid was not pleased. He berated Malka for her simple diet and told her she must eat rich foods, meats with wine, at her meals from now on. She was a wealthy woman and must eat according to her station in life.

Malka, though surprised, agreed to the Maggid's request and left with the Rabbi's blessing.

The Maggid's disciples, who had stood by watching, were also surprised.

"Rabbi," they asked, "why did you tell her to eat rich foods? What does it matter if she eats bread and salt and water, or meats and wines? And isn't it better not to indulge oneself but to live with simple ways and simple pleasures?"

"Ah, one might think so," answered the rabbi. "But if a wealthy person is accustomed to eating and being satisfied with only a little bread and salt and water, then when a poor man comes to her door asking for food, she may expect the poor man to survive on stones. Let the rich one be accustomed to meats and wines. Then, at least, she'll give the poor man some bread and salt and water."

5
Creating Angels

ev was on his way home. His rabbi had sent him to study in the distant town of Lutsk, and now he was eager to see his family and home once again. He had not been sent to study Torah, or *Mishnah*, or *Gemara*, for these he knew well. No, he had been sent to learn a simple lesson from a simple *hasid*—how to trust in God.

He was thinking of how he would tell his rabbi all that he had learned when suddenly, he heard shouts and cries. He ran over to a small group of people to see what was the matter. To his horror, he saw two women bound in chains being dragged by three guards. And even worse, their children ran after them, calling for them and weeping. It was the kind of sight that would soften the heart of any human being, except those three guards.

Lev called to one of the women. "Tell me. What has happened?"

"Our husbands ran the village inn," said one, who talked fast to keep up with the burly guards. "They couldn't pay their rent on time. So afraid were they of the landlord that they ran away."

"The landlord had us arrested instead. We are to be killed!" said the other, her head turned all the while toward her children's cries.

Lev stopped the guards. "Please, take me to the landlord. I want to pay their rent."

The three guards, the two shackled women, the screaming children, and Lev all turned around. When they reached the landlord's house, they found he was not at home, but his agent was.

"Here is 150 rubles, for that is all I carry with me," Lev said to the agent. "I will write a note that will be good for the rest, and as soon as I am home, I will send it."

"That won't do," said the agent. "You have to give me every ruble that is owed right now. The landlord is very angry at those two who ran away. We will be lucky if he accepts even that."

So Lev put all his coins on the table, from every pocket. He had to sell his watch and his coat and his best leather boots. But he managed to come up with every ruble needed. The women were freed and led their children home, with many thanks to Lev.

Lev took to the road again, a much rougher and colder road without his coat and boots. Yet he was grateful to God that he had been able to save the two women.

Finally, Lev stopped at an inn for a rest. He had no money to rent a room, but the kind innkeeper let him sit in front of the fire and rest his feet on a low table. A merchant had stopped at the inn too and sat near Lev to be by the fire.

They chatted about this and that. Lev told the man where he came from and where he was going.

"Then you will pass near the village of Brisk on your way home," said the merchant.

Lev nodded in agreement.

"Would you do me a favor?" asked the merchant. "I am never near Brisk and I have some money that needs to be delivered to my cousin there. Our uncle died and left no children, so each of us inherited a share. I would be so grateful if you would save me this trip."

"Of course," answered Lev. "It is not far out of the way."

"And please accept this money for your service."

"Oh, I cannot," protested Lev, but the man insisted.

The two men talked through the night. The next morning, Lev made ready to leave the inn and sewed the cousin's coins into the hem of his shirt for safety. With the merchant's gift to him, he bought a coat and boots and was looking forward once again to seeing his family and home at his journey's end.

But first he had to deliver the inheritance. When he reached Brisk, he mentioned the cousin's name here and there, at the butcher shop, the tailor's, the soap-maker's. It was a big town, but not that big. Surely someone had heard of this cousin. Yet no one had.

How strange, thought Lev. Surely I have not made a mistake. He did say Brisk.

Lev stayed for one day, two, three, until there was not a soul he had not asked.

He left Brisk feeling the heavy weight of the coins that were not his. If only he had taken the merchant's name and address. There was only one thing to do. He would ask the rabbi.

In a few days, Lev reached his family and home. All were delighted to see him and hear of his adventures. As soon as he could manage, Lev ran off to see his rabbi. He told him of the lessons he had learned, of the two poor women, of the merchant, the inheritance, and the missing cousin.

He ended his tale by jingling the coins that were still in his shirt hem and throwing up his hands. "What am I to do now?" he asked. "I have failed the merchant and deprived the cousin of his inheritance."

Much to Lev's surprise, the rabbi leaned back in his chair and smiled warmly at him. "You have learned your simple lesson well," he said. "To do what needs to be done and to trust in the Holy One. As for the money, it is yours."

"But . . . but . . . I do not understand, Rabbi," mumbled Lev.

"There is a reason you could not find the cousin," answered the rabbi. "There is no cousin and no inheritance. The man you met at the inn was not a man but an angel.

"Something happens when we perform a *mitzvah* like the one you did when you paid the debt and so saved two women from death," the rabbi explained. "Angels are created by these good deeds, our good deeds.

"The merchant was an angel, created by your *mitzvah*. And so the money is meant for you. Use it well and with great joy."

6
The Unusual
Innkeeper

wo merchants traveled by wagon together to the fair in Brody and made ready to leave in time to be home for the Sabbath. On their way, they stopped at an inn for a short rest. Aharon, the innkeeper, invited them to stay for the Sabbath, but the merchants refused, believing that he was interested in them only for their money.

The two merchants had not traveled far from the inn, however, when one of their wagon wheels collapsed. The driver ran back to the inn to buy another wheel.

"Please bring those travelers here," said Aharon. "It's getting late, and they might not make it home before sundown."

When the two reluctant merchants returned to the inn, Aharon welcomed them. "I am so glad you have taken my advice and returned," he said. "And so there will be no misunderstandings, I always tell people before the Sabbath begins that I will charge them each five gold coins at Sabbath's end for their stay. I know this sounds a bit expensive, but for that you may order the best food and wine I have to offer. May your stay be a pleasant one."

Despite Aharon's gracious manner, his words convinced the merchants that they had been right all along. He *was* only interested in filling his inn with customers and earning more money.

"It looks as if we have no choice but to stay here," said one of the merchants, after Aharon himself showed them to their rooms. "We might as well relax and enjoy the most expensive dishes and wines he has."

And that they did. They ate and drank, walked to the town's little synagogue to pray, and studied and sang Sabbath songs with the innkeeper and his family.

"It is almost worth the price," said one merchant to the other when the Sabbath was over.

"You are right. I feel rested and well taken care of," said the other. "Yet I still resent this innkeeper's way of increasing his business by making use of the day of rest."

The two merchants packed their belongings and went to Aharon to pay the five gold coins each that they owed him.

To their surprise, Aharon would not accept the coins.

"I do not want your money," explained Aharon. "You were my guests for the Sabbath and no Sabbath guest here pays for his food and lodging."

"But . . . but . . . " sputtered one of the merchants. "You said you would charge us each five gold coins at Sabbath's end."

Aharon smiled. "That is only my way of making sure each Sabbath guest orders only the best from my inn. For if you believed you were not paying for any of it, you would not have treated yourselves as well as you did."

The stunned merchants left Aharon's inn with a whole new opinion of the innkeeper and his ways.

7
The Fragrance of Good Deeds

efore Rabbi Mordechai became a rabbi, he was a shoemaker. Mostly he mended a hole here and fixed a sole there because few villagers could afford new shoes. When he was a poor shoemaker, and later when he was a famous rabbi, this Mordechai was well-known for his sense of humor.

Although he made very little as a shoemaker, Rabbi Mordechai always managed to save some money for each holiday. He would buy *matzah* and wine for Passover, cheese for Shavuot, a round *hallah* bread for Rosh Hashanah, and a *lulav* and *etrog* for Sukkot.

An *etrog* was not cheap. Coming all the way from the Holy Land, the yellow, lemonlike fruit brought high prices in the marketplace. Each year, Rabbi Mordechai looked forward to inspecting all the *etrogim* in the market stalls and selecting the most perfect one. There must be no blemish, a nice shape, and smooth skin.

The *etrogim* always lent a spicy smell to the marketplace, a special aroma that reminded Rabbi Mordechai of the old saying that good deeds have the fragrance of rare spices.

A few days before Sukkot, Rabbi Mordechai closed his shop and traveled to Brody, the nearest city. In his purse, he carried the coins he had so carefully put aside for the *etrog*.

He looked forward to buying his *etrog* and holding it next to his tall palm branch on the holiday. He thought about how he would shake the *lulav* and *etrog* in the four directions, above and below. The sound of the waving was like the wind passing through the autumn wheat.

As he neared the city, Rabbi Mordechai saw a wagon stranded by the side of the road. Coming closer, he heard a man crying.

"What happened?" he asked the man.

"An accident. My horse. It's dead." The man spoke haltingly, trying to catch his breath. "How am I to make a living?" he sobbed.

Rabbi Mordechai stood by the dejected man, sadly eyeing the dead horse and the toppled wagon.

An *etrog* for Sukkot, that is a commandment from God, the rabbi thought. But *tzedakah*, charity, is also a commandment from God. Rabbi Mordechai made a decision. He reached into his purse and handed his *etrog* money to the man, every penny.

"Buy yourself another horse," he said. "And may you prosper."

Feeling joyful at being able to help another, the rabbi turned around and traveled back to his town of Neschiz.

When he returned home, the villagers crowded around him to see his *etrog*. Not many could afford to buy their own. They would have to use the community-owned *etrog*.

"Can we see your *etrog*?" they asked.

"Is it a beauty like last year's?"

"May we borrow it?"

"Sh," said Rabbi Mordechai, waving his hand up and down to quiet his friends. "There is something I must tell you."

And Rabbi Mordechai told the story of his trip to Brody, of the weeping man and the dead horse. With a very serious look on his face, he said, "On Sukkot, Jews all over the world will say the blessing over the *etrog*—everybody, that is, except for me. I have been granted the rare privilege of saying the blessing over a dead horse!"

The good rabbi chuckled at the astonished looks on his friends' faces, but soon they too found themselves smiling.

8
Mud Makes the Difference

abbi Israel was accustomed to traveling from village to village so that all his disciples could visit with him and learn from him.

When Rabbi Israel visited Dovid's town, Dovid was pleased to host the rabbi in all ways—to serve him the finest foods, provide him with the best linens. There was one thing, however, that bothered Dovid. So many of the rabbi's disciples would come in and out of his house with muddy boots that the floors had to be scrubbed three times a day.

When Dovid approached the rabbi with this one complaint, the rabbi sat him down for a story.

"There once was a poor family traveling by wagon," began Rabbi Israel. "The road was very muddy, and before they knew it, the poor family's wagon got stuck in a ditch and toppled over. Fortunately, no one was hurt, but they were all covered with mud, and their wagon was a pile of broken pieces.

"On this same road, coming in the opposite direction, was a wealthy man in a fancy carriage. Now this wealthy man was usually not very kind or generous to the poor who came to his door. He ordered his servants to turn them away when they asked for food or coins or a bed. But here he was in the out-of-doors, and he found he could not ignore the despair and sorrow on the faces of the poor farmer, his wife, and three small children. He ordered his driver to stop, and both he and the driver helped the poor family climb into his fancy carriage. They loaded the family's goods on top of the carriage and hitched the horse to the back. Then they drove the family home. The wealthy man even gave the poor farmer enough money to buy a new wagon.

"Years later, when the wealthy man died, he was called up to the Heavenly Court to account for his deeds—the good and the bad. The enormous golden scales of justice tipped very definitely on the side of his bad deeds. After all, he had been a wealthy man and had chosen not to help all the poor souls who knocked on his door.

"Are there any other deeds, good or bad, that we have overlooked?" asked the head angel, "before we pronounce a final judgment on this man's soul?"

"May I speak?" said an angel. "As you well know, many of us in this court came into being because of the good deeds performed by those on earth. I was created when this man helped a poor farmer and his family."

"Come, then," ordered the head angel. "Place the family on the scales and see if they balance out this man's bad deeds."

The angel flew out and returned with a most surprised farmer, farmer's wife, and children. The family added a great weight to the side of the scales that represented the good man's deeds, but alas, not enough to even balance the scales, let alone tip them in the wealthy man's favor.

"Wait just a few minutes more," said the angel. She flew away a second time. When she returned, she carried a box filled with mud.

"This is the mud that covered the wealthy man when he helped the poor farmer and his family. And the mud the farmer and his family brought into the fine carriage with them when the wealthy man took them home."

All the members of the Heavenly Court and the rich man, the farmer, his wife, and children watched with interest as the angel placed the mud on the good-deeds side of the scales. Slowly, slowly, the scales shifted. First, all watched as the two sides balanced. Then with the last bit of mud, the scales tipped in the wealthy man's favor.

"Since this man's good deed now outweighs his bad ones," announced the head angel, "his soul will be allowed to enter Paradise."

With this, Rabbi Israel's story ended, and Dovid did not need to hear another word. He had learned the rabbi's lesson, and never again would he complain about the mud on the boots of the rabbi's disciples.

9
The Two Beggars

here were two beggars who wandered the streets of the city together each day collecting coins. When they passed by the palace, the Queen herself often gave them each a loaf of bread. And each time she did so, the beggars would say the same thing.

One, taller than the other and younger, would say, "Oh, Queen. You are so generous and kind."

The other beggar, shorter and with more gray hairs in his beard, said, "Thank You, God, Ruler of the Universe, who has been so generous to this earthly Queen and enables her to help me."

Day after day, the words of the second beggar annoyed the Queen. She thought herself mighty and powerful and knew of no such Ruler of the Universe. She decided upon a plan that would teach this beggar to reconsider his words and his thank-yous.

Going first to her storeroom and then to her kitchens, the Queen told her baker, "Today you are to bake two loaves that look exactly the same. In the middle of one, you are to put these precious stones that are in my hand." The Queen held out a palmful of dazzling rubies and emeralds.

"In the middle of the other loaf, you are to put nothing. When the two beggars come, make sure you give the bread with the jewels to the taller, younger beggar, for he knows how to give thanks properly and to praise the Queen. The ordinary loaf goes to the shorter, older beggar, for I do not wish to reward him in any way."

The baker made the two loaves of bread exactly as the Queen commanded. When the two beggars appeared at the palace entrance the next day, the baker carefully handed the one with the jewels to the younger beggar and the empty loaf to the older.

As he left the palace, the younger beggar could not help but notice that his bread was very heavy. Surely, this loaf is poorly baked, he thought. He turned to his fellow beggar and asked him if he would exchange loaves. The older beggar, always eager to be helpful and friendly, agreed. Then they each went to their own poor hut.

When the older beggar sat down to break his bread at his table, the glittering jewels spilled out of the loaf and onto the dirt floor about him. Quickly, he picked them up, exclaiming, "Thank You, O Ruler of the Universe, for being so generous to me, Your humble servant. Now I will never have to beg again. I will show my gratitude by being as kind to every beggar I see as You have been to me."

Of course, when the younger beggar sat down at his table and broke his bread, all he found was bread.

The next day, the taller, younger beggar waited for his fellow beggar. Since he did not come, the younger beggar wandered the streets alone and appeared at the palace entrance as usual. The Queen was very surprised to see the younger beggar at her door.

"Did you not get your bread yesterday?" the Queen asked.

"Yes. But the baker gave me a heavy and poorly baked loaf, so I exchanged it with my friend, who was very willing to give me his finely baked one."

The Queen was silent. She understood now that the old beggar was right. All riches do come from this Ruler of the Universe. An earthly king or queen, though with some might and power, cannot always affect the fortunes of another, even a beggar. And a person's plans, though she might be a queen, are not above God's.

10
Ox and Herbs

here was a bitter time during King Solomon's rule when he was banished from his very own kingdom by the evil and jealous King of the Demons, Asmodeus. For three years, King Solomon wandered among strangers, a common beggar. No one in this faraway place recognized him.

When King Solomon tried to tell his story, people laughed at him. One look at his tattered clothes, his dirty, unshaven face, and people thought these were the ravings of a madman.

There were two times, however, in this far-off land that Solomon was recognized as the King he really was. When he regained his throne from the wicked Asmodeus, Solomon told about these times.

"Once, as I begged from house to house, I met a very wealthy man. He was a Jewish merchant who carried goods in caravans from one place to another. He knew me for who I was, as he had often traveled to Jerusalem.

"He invited me to a sumptuous dinner, roasted ox and the finest of vegetables, honeyed sweets and nuts. Yet each time I took a bite, he would bemoan my fate.

"'How could a king fall so low as to be a beggar?' he would say. 'How meager is this meal compared to the feasts you had in your own palace!' With every word, he reminded me of what I had lost.

"He invited me back more than once, but I could not go. For none of his wonderful food could I taste or even swallow.

"In the marketplace, I met the other man, a vendor of herbs and onions. He had once supplied the palace kitchens with herbs but left the city to seek his fortune elsewhere. He was much poorer than when I last saw him, yet he too invited me to his home to eat.

"'I am sorry this is all I have to offer you,' said my poor friend when he placed a dish of simple greens before me.

"We sat and ate together. And each time my friend saw me pause in my eating, a look of sadness crossing my face, he consoled me.

"'Oh, King, do not despair. God will surely restore you to your throne. Do you not remember God's promise to your father, King David? God said that the royal line will spring forth from your father's seed. See, you *will* return to Jerusalem!'

"So," said Solomon, "the meal of simple herbs and warm advice that the market vendor provided satisfied me much more than the rich meal of oxen and woe that the wealthy man gave to me."

And this is how King Solomon explained the proverb "Better a meager meal where there is love than a feast where there is hatred" (Proverbs 15:17).

11
The Kaddish

ryeh Lev was a good student. So, even though they were poor, his parents sent him off to study in a famous *yeshivah*, a school for the advanced study of the holy books.

"We will find a way for him to stay here," promised the *yeshivah* rabbi.

He gave Aryeh Lev a note addressed to Reb Shmuel, one of the wealthiest men in the town, asking him to provide Aryeh Lev with his meals. This was not unusual, for most of the *yeshivah* students came from poor families and were invited to eat at different houses each night. It was considered a great *mitzvah* to feed the *yeshivah* students.

As Aryeh Lev walked along, he dreamed of all the fine meals he would eat at this Reb Shmuel's house. Soups and stews, beef and cabbage, honey cakes and fruit-filled cookies. However, when Aryeh Lev delivered the rabbi's letter, the wealthy man acted indignant. Instead of offering his own hospitality, he gave Aryeh Lev the names of other householders to ask.

Embarrassed by Reb Shmuel's manner, Aryeh Lev decided not to ask anyone else but to live on bread alone. He used the little bit of money his parents were able to send him.

One evening, on his way to the baker's to buy his bread, Aryeh Lev was stopped by an elderly woman. "I am collecting money to free an innocent man who has been arrested on false charges," she said.

"I am sorry I do not have more to give you," Aryeh Lev said, handing her a few coins.

"Oh, I am the one who is sorry," she said. "I can see how little you have yourself." And she handed Aryeh Lev back his coins, adding a few more of her own.

"No, I insist," he said and gave all the coins to the woman. "It is not every day I have a chance to participate in such a *mitzvah*."

"In that case, I will accept your coins," said the woman, "if you will take mine as payment for saying the mourner's prayer, the *Kaddish*, for my late husband. Tonight is the anniversary of his death, his *yahrzeit*, and my son is unable to recite the prayer."

Aryeh Lev gladly agreed and went directly to the synagogue for the evening service, where he said *Kaddish*. He stayed a bit longer and also studied some verses in Talmud for the benefit of the husband's soul and the souls of the others whose *yahrzeits* were that night.

When he left the synagogue, he headed once again to the baker's for his loaf of bread. Again he was interrupted in his errand, this time by an old man who walked stooped over and with the help of a gold-tipped cane.

"I want to thank you for the *Kaddish* you recited at the synagogue and for the verses of Talmud you studied this night," said the man. "Please take this note. It is addressed to a close friend of mine who will provide you with all that you need while you study at the *yeshivah*. You will deliver my note?"

"Of course, sir. I am very grateful to you," said Aryeh Lev as he pocketed the note.

I will open it later, after the baker's, he thought, and continued on his original errand.

His loaf eaten, Aryeh Lev perched on his bed at the *yeshivah*. With a great deal of excitement, he took out the old man's paper. But when he opened the note, all his hopes vanished, all his dreams of regular hot meals to come. For the note was addressed to the very same Reb Shmuel that Aryeh Lev had visited before.

The next day after his classes, Aryeh Lev reluctantly knocked at Reb Shmuel's door.

"It's you again," Reb Shmuel said when he saw Aryeh Lev. "Did you not go to the householders whose names I gave you?"

"Excuse me, sir," said Aryeh Lev, hoping to avoid the question. "An old man told me to give you this."

Reb Shmuel took the note. As he read it, his hands began to tremble, and he looked at Aryeh Lev in an odd way.

"You say an old man gave you this?"

"Yes, I met him in the street, sir. Last night. He thanked me for the *Kaddish* I said."

"You said *Kaddish*? For whom?" Reb Shmuel asked, his voice rising so that Aryeh Lev trembled too.

"Well, you see," Aryeh Lev answered haltingly. "Before the old man, I met a woman who paid me to say *Kaddish* for her late husband. She said her son was not able to."

Reb Shmuel stood for a moment in silence, staring first at the note and then at Aryeh Lev and past him.

"Would you recognize this old man if you saw him again?" he asked Aryeh Lev at last, his voice a little calmer now.

"I think so," said Aryeh Lev.

"Then come with me."

Aryeh Lev followed the man to a nearby room full of comfortable stuffed chairs and sofas. Portraits hung on one wall.

"Do you recognize the old man here? In any of these portraits?" asked Reb Shmuel.

"Why, yes. That one there," said Aryeh Lev. "He even holds the same gold-tipped cane."

Reb Shmuel crumpled down into one of the soft chairs and sobbed.

Aryeh Lev waited, not at all sure of what he should do.

At last, Reb Shmuel looked up at him. "That old man you met on the street was my late father and that woman is my mother. My father died ten years ago, and I am sorry to say, I did not even remember his *yahrzeit*. I have been so busy with my own affairs that I have neglected both my father's memory and my mother's wishes.

"At first, I thought you had returned with a trick, a gimmick, to get me to support you in your studies. But now I know this is not a gimmick. You could not know how to duplicate my father's handwriting, or know what he looked like, or remember that last night was his *yahrzeit*. No. Even after these ten years, I cannot help but recognize that this note is in my father's own writing."

Reb Shmuel got up from the chair, slowly and thoughtfully. "Wait here," he told Aryeh Lev.

In a few minutes he returned and handed Aryeh Lev the amount of money his father had written on the note. "Thank you for saying *Kaddish* for my father," he said.

From then on, Reb Shmuel completely changed. He became a caring and generous person and a loving son. He also became one of the prime supporters of not only the famous *yeshivah* but of Aryeh Lev as well. No more plain bread for dinner. Now Aryeh Lev ate soups and stews, roast beef and cabbage, honey cakes and fruit-filled cookies at the home of Reb Shmuel every single night.

12
The Loan

poor woman named Razel once came to the rabbi for a loan. She was a widow with eight children to support, and now her youngest, Yidel, had taken sick.

The rabbi, seeing Razel's great need, gave her the money she asked for, and together they set a date for the repayment of the loan in a year's time.

A year came and went, and there was no sign of any repayment from Razel.

The rabbi's bookkeeper, Hillel, wanted to go himself to collect what Razel owed. But the rabbi stopped him.

"Razel is an honest woman," said the rabbi. "If she hasn't come to repay her loan, she must be in even worse circumstances than before. Here, take this and give it to her."

The rabbi put a large sum of money into Hillel's hand for Razel.

Now a couple of years passed. One day, Razel appeared at the rabbi's house. "I am sorry, Rabbi. It has taken me so long, but I have finally come to repay my loan," she said. And Razel held out the money.

The rabbi stared for a second at her cracked and work-worn hand.

"Oh, that," the rabbi said. "I am sorry. I cannot accept it."

"Oh, you must, Rabbi," said Razel. "It is such a great sum. And we agreed."

"We did. But you see," said the rabbi, "in my mind, I gave up any claim to that money a long time ago. Please, keep your hard-earned money, Razel. I know you will use it well."

13
The Rabbi's Blessing

nce, in Tunisia long ago, there lived a rabbi whose habit was to study Torah nightly by the light of a small oil lamp. On one particularly windy night, as the rabbi studied, a draft came and snuffed out his light. The rabbi lit the cotton wick and resumed his study. *Whoosh.* A draft extinguished his light a second time. And a third time.

By now, the rabbi had no matches left to relight his wick, and so, despite the lateness of the hour, he decided to go ask his neighbor, the baker, for a match.

When he knocked on the baker's door, the Arab apprentice Ali answered. Hearing the rabbi's problem, he gladly gave him a lit piece of wood, a brand, to carry back to his house and so light his lamp.

On the rabbi's way back, however, the rain and wind snuffed this fire out too.

"Whatever evil forces abound this night," the rabbi muttered, "trying to trick me into giving up my study of Torah—you will find that I do not give up so easily!"

Much as he disliked waking the apprentice yet another time, the rabbi made his way back to the baker's and knocked again.

To the apprentice's credit, he amiably fetched a second brand for the rabbi. As he watched the rabbi walk out into the stormy night, though, the apprentice stopped him. "Perhaps I had better go with you to see that this fire does not go out."

Ali carried the brand himself and kept it dry by shielding it with a board. Then he relit the rabbi's oil lamp and stayed for a time to make sure it did not go out.

"May God bless you," the grateful rabbi said to Ali. "May as much money come into your hands as there are grains of sand on the seashore."

The rest of the night passed peacefully. Ali went back to his bed, the rabbi resumed his studies, and the lamp stayed lit throughout the night.

The next morning, after finishing his work in the bakery, Ali went to the coffeehouse, as was his custom. He met a tall, strange man there who greeted him and asked him to come work for him. "I will pay you more than you earn now," the stranger promised. "I have just one request—that you wear this blindfold when I lead you to my house."

And so the stranger led Ali through the streets and inside his house, where he removed the blindfold. "Let me show you where you will work."

The man bent down over a wooden handle attached to a marble slab in the floor. When he pulled on the handle, the marble moved, revealing a hole in the floor. In the small hidden room underneath lay thousands and thousands of gold and silver coins.

"This is why I asked you to wear the blindfold—because of all the money I keep in my house," said the stranger. "Your job will be to sort and count the coins and tie them up into these sacks."

Ali did as he was asked. When evening came, the man returned with a plentiful meal for Ali and also his day's wages.

The next day was much the same as the first, and so it went for two years. Ali was glad for the better wages. Still he could not help but wish that the rabbi's blessing had spoken not of money coming into his hands but of his owning it.

When the coins were all sorted, his employer gave Ali a whole year's extra wages and wished him well.

Ali was free to walk about town and sit in the coffeehouse. His pockets were full of money—for the time being.

One day, as Ali sat in the coffeehouse, the town crier came by. "House for sale. Fine house for sale," he called.

Ali stopped him. "Who does this fine house belong to?"

"To a man who just died," said the crier. "That is all I know. I've just been hired to announce the sale of the house and everything in it."

I wonder if this house could belong to the tall man I worked for, thought Ali. "I will pay five hundred pounds for it," Ali said aloud.

"I will pay six hundred," said another coffeehouse customer.

"A thousand," said Ali.

"A thousand and five hundred," said the other.

I have to buy that house, thought Ali, for if it is the tall man's, I'll be rich. And if not, I'll be as poor as I was when I started. But that is fate. And so he said, "Two thousand."

"No more," said the other bidder.

"Sold for two thousand pounds," the crier said to Ali.

When Ali paid the two thousand, about all the money that he had, he was given the key and address of the house. His fate in his hands, he walked up and down the twisting streets until he came to the house he had bought. Once inside, he knew the house to be the tall man's, for there was the marble slab with the wooden handle on the floor. But would the gold and silver coins still be there?

Ali bent down and pulled on the wooden handle. The marble slab moved to reveal the treasure. Ali was a rich man!

Taking some of the sacks of coins with him, Ali covered over the hidden room and left the house. Quietly, he bought a rug here, a piece of jewelry there, some cloth, and loaded all his puchases onto a wagon that he brought to Egypt. There he sold all the goods for a handsome profit. He did the same thing again and again—returning to the hidden room for coins, buying goods, and traveling to Egypt to sell them for a profit.

Ali bought himself a fine house in Egypt and more and more goods and shops until he owned almost the whole town and was chosen as its mayor.

The years that passed for Ali passed also for the rabbi, who forgot all about the night that his candle blew out. He continued to immerse himself in his studies and tend to his congregation. His wish, to spend his last years in the Holy City, in Jerusalem, grew stronger as he grew older.

Finally, the day came that the rabbi was to leave on his journey to the Holy Land. His congregation, though a poor one, made sure he did not travel alone. They sent him off with food and books and a troop of nine young men, enough to form, counting the rabbi, a prayer group, a *minyan*. Once he was in Jerusalem, then he would have to find his own way.

In their travels east toward Jerusalem, they passed through many cities and towns, orchards and fields, until they reached Ali's own town in Egypt.

There they stopped and sat under some shade trees eating their lunch, when a beautiful carriage came by. To their amazement, the carriage halted before them, and a man dressed in the richest robes stepped down. He walked over to the rabbi and kissed his hand.

"Who are you to bow before me and kiss my hand?" asked the rabbi, perplexed.

"You do not recognize me?" said the rich man. "I recognize you. You were the rabbi of the town where I grew up in Tunisia, though, of course, I was not a part of your congregation. Yet all that I have today, I owe to you. Come by my house tomorrow. I have much to show you and to tell you."

"Will we go?" one of the rabbi's young men asked, as soon as the rich man's carriage had driven away.

"For a little while," answered the rabbi. "I'm curious to·know why this wealthy Arab gentleman should think all his riches are due to me!"

So the next day, the rabbi and his entourage went to this rich man's house. Ali took the rabbi from one room to another, showing him woven rugs and jars of oils, bolts of cloth, and gold and silver.

"What great wealth God has given you!" exclaimed the rabbi, who had never seen such riches.

"It is not only mine," answered his guide. "It is yours as well, Rabbi. Do you still not know who I am? I am Ali, the baker's apprentice, who helped you light your oil lamp on that stormy night long ago. You blessed me with wealth, and Heaven made your blessing come true. It is because of you that I am the richest man in all of Egypt!"

"Ali, the baker's apprentice?" the rabbi repeated. "Yes, of course I remember now. Such blessings! It is a wonderful thing!"

"I wish to share them with you, Rabbi," said Ali. "From now on, I will pay all the expenses of your journey."

"It is not everyone who chooses to be generous with blessings once they receive them," the rabbi said. "I am most grateful to you."

The two embraced, and the rabbi once more set out on his journey, this time supported by his wealthy friend. In Jerusalem, he was able to establish a great school of Torah learning. And each month, ten camels loaded with wheat, barley, olive oil, gold and silver came from Egypt, sent, of course, by the most faithful and gracious Ali.

14
The Watchman

ochanan lived at the edge of his town, and perhaps because of his location, people often came to his door. Some merely needed directions, others a warm meal or a place to stay, for the trek down the windy isolated road from the next village was a very long one.

Yochanan considered himself fortunate to be able to help others in this way and never missed an opportunity to offer his hospitality to the wayfarer. He even went out of his way to do so.

One very cold night, in the middle of winter, Yochanan looked out his window and saw several merchants passing by his house, their wagons loaded high with goods.

He opened his door and called out to them. "There is no inn for miles. Please, come inside. The snow is falling heavily and the wind howls so. You can stay here for the night."

"That is very kind of you," said one of the merchants, "but we don't want to leave all our goods outside unguarded."

"You needn't worry," answered Yochanan. "The night watchman will look after your wagons."

The merchants, much relieved, thanked Yochanan. While they settled their wagons and horses for the night, Yochanan fixed their sleeping places and heated a hearty soup on the big wood stove.

They came in from the cold, stamping the snow off their boots and undoing their heavy coats and scarves and hats.

"The night watchman has not yet come," said one of the merchants to Yochanan. "Perhaps we should stay outside a little longer."

"Oh, no need," answered Yochanan. "I know he will be here very soon."

Yochanan served them the soup and showed them their beds.

"Good night," he called from his little room. "And don't worry. I see the night watchman coming now." Then quietly Yochanan dressed in his warmest clothes and slipped out the back door of his house. For there was no night watchman. Only Yochanan.

15
A Town of Baruchs

oshe was a wealthy businessman, well loved in his town, for not only was he wealthy but he was also kind and generous. If a family could not pay their rent and would soon be thrown out onto the street, there was Moshe to help them. If a businessman suffered a fire and did not have the money to rebuild his store, Moshe helped him too.

Moshe and his wife, Rifka, had their wealth and their good health, their loving friends, and their business to keep them busy. But in their fifteen years of marriage, they had never had a child. And this they wanted very much.

One evening, as they often did, Moshe and Rifka talked about their longing.

"I do not understand it," said Moshe. "I know the Baal Shem Tov, our wonder-working rabbi, cares much for us. But whenever I ask him to bless us with a child, he blesses us instead with prosperity and wealth. Now,

I'm thankful for the prosperity and wealth, of course. But it is so lonely, so painful, not to have a child."

"I know," said Rifka. "I feel the pain too. Perhaps we should travel to the rabbi once more and ask him together."

So Moshe and Rifka left the very next day to seek out their rabbi with their request.

The Baal Shem Tov welcomed them warmly and listened to them carefully.

"It is as if we will have left no impression on the world," explained Moshe. "There will be no children to mourn for us after we die; no children to keep our memory alive."

"No one to care for," added Rifka. "To love and be loved back."

"I think you will find your answer to this request if you come with me on a trip," said the Baal Shem. "I wish you to see a little town that is a five-day journey from here."

Moshe and Rifka were puzzled but were curious to see how this town could provide them with an answer. A town is not a baby, after all.

For five days, Moshe and Rifka, the Baal Shem Tov, and several of his disciples traveled by horse and carriage through the countryside of Poland until they reached a little town near Brody.

At the town water pump, they saw a group of children. Some were filling buckets with water, and others were splashing about in the puddles around the pump.

"What is your name?" the Baal Shem asked the tallest boy.

"Baruch Shlomo," was his reply.

"And yours?" he asked of another boy.

"The same. Baruch Shlomo," came the answer.

There were one, two, three, four, five, six Baruch Shlomos in the group. A Baruch Yermiyahu and a Baruch Adam too.

A little girl by the pump spoke up without having to be asked. "My name is Bracha Leah, Baruch Adam's sister."

Moshe and Rifka were quite surprised. So many Baruch Shlomos! Such a coincidence.

They went on walking, surprise adding to surprise.

They stopped each child they met and asked their names.

There were five Baruch Shlomos outside the *heder*, the school, and three more by the blacksmith's shop. There were two by the market stalls, plus four Bracha Leahs. And a Shlomo Matisyahu and a Shlomo Eliezer and a Leah Esther too, running errands for their mothers.

Everywhere they went in this strange town were Baruch Shlomos and Bracha Leahs, and Shlomo thises and Leah thats.

"Surely there was a great scholar-rabbi who lived here by the name of Baruch Shlomo," Moshe whispered to his wife.

"Yes. And his wife, a great righteous lady with the name of Bracha Leah," she whispered back.

They prayed in the town's little wooden synagogue that afternoon. When the prayers were over, the Baal Shem brought Moshe and Rifka over to an old man who was sitting on a bench by one wall.

"My friends are wondering why almost all the children here have the same names," said the Baal Shem. "Could you tell them the reason?"

The man smiled. "People always ask us that," he said. "There is a good reason, if you have a minute."

"Oh, we do," said Moshe and Rifka and the Baal Shem and all his disciples. They pulled up a few more benches near the old man.

"Many years ago," began the old man, "there was a wealthy butcher in our town. He had one son. The father was not only a butcher but a learned man who knew the Torah by heart and did good deeds by the dozens. His son, though a good man, was not a scholar. Yet he did have a business head on his shoulders. And he too was full of good deeds. That much his father had been able to teach him. The father's name was Avram Yosaf. The son's was Baruch Shlomo."

Moshe lifted up his finger and opened his mouth as if to say something, but the old man interrupted him. "Yes, Baruch Shlomo," he repeated.

"When he grew up, the son took over the butcher shop completely. His father was able to spend all his time studying and learning. Baruch Shlomo married a good woman, Bracha Leah."

Again his listeners recognized the name, but they kept quiet, not wanting to disturb the old man's story.

"They had a good life, this Baruch Shlomo and Bracha Leah, but alas, no children," continued the old man. "Then Baruch Shlomo's father died. And soon his mother too. Baruch Shlomo very much wanted to honor his parents' memory and decided the best way to do this would be to study and learn as his father did.

"Maybe now that he was older, studying would come easier to him, Baruch Shlomo reasoned.

"So he worked at the butcher shop during the day and went to the *Beit Hamidrash*, the House of Study, at night. But try as he did, not one piece of learning, not one *mishnah* or *pasuk*, would stay in his head.

"He gave up trying to learn and would sit at the side of the teacher, listening to every word he said, hoping some of the learning would stick.

"One day Baruch Shlomo heard the teacher say, 'If someone teaches Torah to another's child, it is as if he were the parent of that child.'

"Now Baruch Shlomo felt even worse. Not only did he have no child of his own, but he would never be able to teach another's child either. He would lose a second chance to be a parent, a second chance to leave someone here on earth after him to remember him and say the mourner's prayer, the *Kaddish*, for him.

"The teacher could sense Baruch Shlomo's despair.

"'Do not be so sad, my friend,' the teacher said. 'You and your wife may still have a child. You are still young.'

"'But I do not know if we will. And one thing I do know is that I cannot teach someone else's child. So I have a double tragedy.' Baruch Shlomo could not keep the tears from coming as he talked.

"'Listen, Baruch Shlomo,' said the teacher. 'There is another meaning to my words. If you provide the means whereby another's child can be taught, it is as if you've taught them yourself.'

"All at once, the teacher's words filled Baruch Shlomo with hope, and he saw what he could do. He couldn't wait to tell Bracha Leah the good news.

"She was as eager as her husband, and so the very next day they both went through the town, gathering up all the children whose parents could not afford to pay any teachers' fees.

"They founded a school for these children and gave extra money to all the other schools in the town. Before long, Baruch Shlomo and Bracha Leah were supporting the education of dozens and dozens of poor children.

"Through the years, they continued to do this. And though they never had any children of their own, they were responsible for educating many. Their butcher shop thrived and they were happy to see 'their children' grow up to be Torah scholars."

Here the old man took a breath and then continued. "The rabbi of our village and I were both educated in the school founded by Baruch Shlomo and Bracha Leah, as were so many others of our generation.

"They have been dead now for fifteen years, having lived a full and rich life and having provided for the continuation of the towns' schools in their wills.

"Many of us whose education we owe to Baruch Shlomo and Bracha Leah have named our children after them. And when the anniversaries of their deaths come each year, we all gather in the synagogue. The rabbi himself leads us in the prayers and in the mourner's *Kaddish* for their immortal souls. They are not forgotten."

When the old man had finished his story, the Baal Shem Tov thanked him.

"Now you see why I wanted you to make this five-day journey with me," he said to Moshe and Rifka.

"I do see," said Rifka. "And we are grateful to you, Rabbi, for bringing us here."

"We know what we must do now," agreed Moshe.

When Moshe and Rifka returned to their store, they felt a new purpose in their lives. They too "adopted" hundreds of children by giving them an education. And they never forgot the village of Baruch Shlomos and Bracha Leahs, that living memorial to a righteous couple's good deeds.

16
The Dirty Pastry

here was once a rich man who guarded every penny he spent and so earned the title "miser." In the marketplace one day, after haggling over the purchase of this and the sale of that, he was hungry and bought a piece of pastry. As he left the market, he tripped and dropped the pastry. It rolled along, and by the time the miser picked it up, it was covered with dirt.

Just then a beggar came by and asked the miser for some coins for food. Instead of handing the beggar coins, the miser handed him the pastry.

That night, when the miser slept, he had a dream, a most vivid dream. He was seated in a cafe. Waiters bustled here and there with trays of delicious sweets and cakes. But they passed right by the miser. Not one waiter stopped at his table. Not one delicious cake was he served.

Finally, he got the attention of one of the waiters and complained. The waiter returned quickly, giving him a piece of dirty pastry.

"This is a disgrace! How can you serve me such dirty pastry?" the miser shouted. "I didn't ask you for charity. I am a wealthy man and can pay for the best."

"I am sorry," answered the waiter. "But here you cannot buy anything with money. You have just entered Eternity. All you can order here is what you have already sent from the time you lived in the earthly world. And since this is all you have sent—a piece of dirty pastry—this is all I am able to serve you."

17
The Rabbi and the Rag Dealer

hen Haim the rag dealer died, the towns-people were very surprised to see the great Berdichever Rebbe at his funeral. The Ber-dichever Rebbe didn't come to everyone's funeral. Why a rag dealer's, even a wealthy rag dealer's?

But then the great rebbe spoke. "I am here because of three lawsuits that came to my rabbinic court involving Haim the rag dealer.

"The first one was many years ago when Haim was a middle-aged man and had worked hard to build up his business. At that time, there was a Jewish man named Avram who had just been released from the Tsar's army. For forty miserable years, Avram served as a soldier. He saved thousands of rubles, which he tied in a red ker-chief to carry with him. With this savings, he hoped to marry and set himself up in a business.

"One day, Avram walked the streets of our town, Berdichev, trying to decide what business he should pursue. That night he took a room at an inn, and when he reached for his kerchief and money, they were gone, lost in the streets somewhere. Now Avram was lost. Early the next morning, he walked to the river, so desolate and downcast that he was prepared to throw himself in.

"Now, in the early mornings, it was Haim the rag dealer's habit to walk along the riverbank to start his day, and he saw this sorrowful-looking man.

"'Is something wrong?' Haim asked Avram.

"'Nothing you can help me with.'

"'Perhaps I can. Tell me.'

"And so Avram told Haim about his red kerchief and his lost money.

"'I can help you,' said Haim happily. 'I found that very same kerchief and money in the streets yesterday and was wondering to whom it belonged. Come back to my house and I'll show you.'

"Now, of course, Haim had not found the man's kerchief. But he took one of his own, wrapped the exact amount of money in it that was lost, and gave all this to Avram.

"Convinced that Haim's kerchief and money were his, Avram felt as happy as the day he'd been discharged from the Tsar's army.

"News traveled quickly thoughout Berdichev about Haim finding Avram's money. That news reached the ears of Peyshe, the very man who had found the real kerchief and money in the street. Haim's good deed gnawed at Peyshe's conscience. He felt worse and worse about keeping the money he had found.

"Eventually, Peyshe went to Haim. He explained that he was the one who had really found the money. But when he tried to give the money to Haim, to repay him for his kind deed, Haim would not take it.

"'This has nothing to do with my money,' said Haim. 'I saw that I could save a man and I did. You take this money and return it to Avram. It is his.'

"So Peyshe brought Haim to court. Imagine! Bringing someone to court because he wouldn't take money! In the end we judged the case in Haim's favor. He did not have to take the money, since it was actually the ex-soldier's.

"Now the second time Haim appeared in my court was a few years later. Of course, I remembered this Haim well, from the first time.

"This time, Yonah, a teacher, appeared in the court with Haim and told this story.

"'I was a poor teacher and wanted to go to another town to see if I could get a better-paying job. But my wife, Rachel, was afraid to let me go. She was worried about how she and our child would live while I was gone. I told her I would arrange for her to borrow five *kopeks* a week from Haim the rag dealer. And she agreed.

"'While I was gone, I realized I had forgotten to make the arrangements with Haim for the loan. So, as soon as I found a job, I hurried home.

"'To my relief, I saw my wife and son were in good health. I asked Rachel how she had managed while I was away.

"'With Haim's five *kopeks* each week, of course,' was her answer. After I explained to Rachel how I had forgotten to make the arrangement with Haim for the loan, the two of us hurried to his house to repay him. Alas, he would not take our money. And that is why I have brought him to your court.'

"Haim told the court that since Yonah had made no arrangement to borrow the five *kopeks* each week, the money was a gift. And Yonah and Rachel could not repay what Haim chose to give as *tzedakah*.

"I could not help but smile at such an odd case," said the rebbe. "Here were two people desperate to give money to someone who refused to take it! But once again the court decided in Haim's favor. *Tzedakah* is *tzedakah*.

"Now the third case. I recognized Haim at once, though this case was many years later, and Haim was by now an old man. Tell me, who could forget such a man as Haim?

"Haim's third appearance in court proved to be as unusual as the first two. After all, in court you usually see people who want money from other people, not people who are trying to give it back.

"This time, Gabriel, a rich man, had come upon hard times and asked Haim to lend him five thousand rubles to start up his business again. Of course, Haim gave him the rubles. The man was so grateful that he said to Haim as he left, 'May God bless you twofold for your kindness.'

"Shortly after, when Haim went to the synagogue to pray, a friend of his told him about a nobleman who had gambled away so much of his money the night before at card playing that he was forced to sell his oxen very cheaply.

"'Buy the oxen,' urged the friend. 'It's a good deal. You have the money.'

"'But I know nothing of oxen,' protested Haim. 'I am a rag dealer.'

"The friend pestered and pestered Haim about the good deal until Haim gave in and bought the oxen from the nobleman for five thousand rubles.

"The oxen proved to be as good a deal as the friend had said. Still knowing nothing of oxen, Haim managed to turn around and sell them that very day for twice as much as he had paid.

"Eventually, this Gabriel reappeared at Haim's house to repay his five-thousand-ruble loan. The loan had helped him, and he was rich once again.

"However, Haim would not take Gabriel's money, so Gabriel brought Haim to our court. 'Please, convince Haim to take his money back,' said Gabriel.

"In his defense, Haim said, 'Gabriel won't listen. After he borrowed the money, he said that God should bless me and repay me twofold for my good deed. That very day, God did this and repaid me with ten thousand rubles. See? Gabriel doesn't owe me anything.'

"If only we had cases such as this one every day,

our worries would be over. For the third time we judged in Haim's favor. We told Gabriel, 'If you really want to give the money back, then use Haim as an example and give it to *tzedakah*.'

"And what an example this Haim the rag dealer was. Now you know why I, the Berdichever Rebbe, have come to Haim the rag dealer's funeral. It is to pay my respects to a most unusual and saintly man."

18
The Tutor's Wages

ehuda was very learned but also very poor. He earned his living by being a tutor.

One winter, he left his family to become a tutor for a wealthy man's son in another village. He hoped to return just before Passover with enough money to buy all those things necessary for the holiday—candles and *matzah*, meats and eggs, and dried fruits and wine.

He tutored through the dark months of winter, but he was not happy, for not only did he miss his family but he became increasingly dismayed at the behavior of his well-to-do employer. The man turned away each and every beggar who came to his door.

Finally, Yehuda could stand this no longer. "Please," he said to the wealthy man, "give these beggars some money. You can deduct what you give them from my wages, if you wish."

His penny-pinching employer readily agreed and kept accounts of all that he gave to the needy ones who came to his door.

As the winter ended, Yehuda made ready to return home. He met with his employer to settle the accounts. First, the employer added up Yehuda's wages. Then he deducted from what Yehuda had earned all that had been given to the poor. Yehuda was left with nothing. No, worse than nothing. He was left owing his employer two gold coins.

And so Yehuda finished his job with even less than he had to begin with. He was not sorry to lose all the money that had been distributed to the poor. But he was sorry to go home empty-handed. How would they celebrate the holiday now?

As he neared his own village, his little son Benyamin ran out to meet him. Yehuda kissed his son and gave him his small bundle of belongings to bring home. "Tell your mother I'll be there soon," Yehuda said, "as soon as I've said my prayers at the synagogue."

Yehuda hurried along. He noticed something shiny on the ground and hesitated but decided not to stop. He would miss the prayers if he did.

A stranger passing by just behind Yehuda picked up the shiny objects, which turned out to be gold coins, and brought them to Yehuda's wife, Gele.

"I think they dropped out of your husband's pockets," he said.

"They're probably my husband's wages," said Gele. "Thank you so much."

After the stranger left, Gele immediately went to the market to buy all that was needed for the holiday.

When Yehuda returned home from synagogue, he was surprised and happy to see his wife preparing the boiled eggs and roasted beef, the mixed nuts and apples, and more. He joined her in the preparation and sent Benyamin off to buy some bitter herbs that Gele had forgotten.

I must remember to ask Gele how she earned enough money to buy all this wonderful food, thought Yehuda.

Benyamin came running back sooner than either of his parents expected with not only the bitter herbs but a story as well.

"I was hurrying down the street to the market," Benyamin said, talking so quickly that his parents had trouble making sense of what he said, "and up ahead was this wagon. I know I shouldn't have, Mama, but I jumped on the back for a ride. I thought, it's right before Passover. Who would mind?

"Then the wagon driver turned around and his face was grim. I didn't know him. I hopped off quickly, afraid he would whip me instead of the horse for my trick.

"But he didn't. Instead, he threw these down at my feet." Benyamin spilled a handful of gold coins onto the table. "And what he said makes no sense."

"What did he say?" Yehuda asked.

"'Add these to your father's wages. And have a good holiday.'"

"That *is* odd," said Yehuda thoughtfully. "Unless. . . ." Suddenly he turned to his wife. "Gele, how did you earn all the money to buy this food?"

"But I didn't earn the money," stammered Gele. "A stranger brought me the coins. He found them on the ground and told me they had fallen out of your pocket. They were your wages, weren't they?"

"Perhaps they were," said Yehuda and smiled. "You know what I think? I think both of your strangers were none other than Elijah the Prophet, come to make sure I didn't return to you empty-handed for the holiday."

"Empty-handed? Elijah the Prophet? What are you talking about?" said Gele. "You earned all that money tutoring, didn't you?"

"Not quite," answered Yehuda. "Sit down and I'll tell you my story."

19
You Know What Friends Are For

or his living, Yidel dug for clay in the forest. Then he loaded the clay onto his wagon and, with his horse's help, delivered the clay to builders, who used it to make bricks. They paid him enough to support his wife and family.

But one day Yidel's horse took sick and died. The townspeople expected Yidel to buy another horse. To their surprise, he didn't. Instead, he walked into the forest, and after he dug the clay, carried it in a box on his own back.

Two of Yidel's neighbors watched him walking by one day.

"Why doesn't Yidel buy another horse?" Sarah said to Hanna.

"He probably doesn't have the money," guessed Hanna.

"Then we'll have to help him," said Sarah. "He won't last long like that."

So Sarah and Hanna went among their friends and took up a collection for Yidel's new horse.

When they had collected enough, they approached Yidel.

"Yidel, we couldn't help but notice," began Hanna.

"You know what friends are for," said Sarah. And they held out the money they'd collected to Yidel.

But Yidel would not lift a hand to take the money.

"I've never taken charity from anyone," said Yidel. "God will help me, as always. Please, friends, take your money and distribute it among the poor."

Hanna looked at Sarah and shrugged.

"If you ever need any help, Yidel, please let us know," said Sarah, and she and Hanna left with the money.

Each day, early in the morning, Yidel's neighbors watched him leave for the forest. And each night he would return, stooped under his heavy load of clay. He earned so little that he could buy only a little. He and his family were always hungry, and Yidel was always tired.

Hanna and Sarah grew afraid for their neighbor.

"How will he continue to live like this?" said Sarah.

"We have to do something," said Hanna.

But what could they do? Nothing. Yidel was too proud to take any money from them.

"If we can't think of any way to help Yidel, I know someone who can," said Hanna. And the two friends went to see Rabbi Levi.

They told him the whole story.

"Leave the money with me," said Rabbi Levi. "I will think of a way."

The rabbi stayed awake that night trying to think of a way to help poor Yidel. Finally, just before dawn, he put on the clothes of a simple laborer and walked to the edge of the forest. There he gathered a large bundle of twigs and strapped them to his back. When he entered the village, he turned down Yidel's street instead of his own. No one paid any attention to the poor twig porter as they hurried to work.

The rabbi dropped the bundle of twigs in front of Yidel's door and left quickly.

Yidel heard the noise of the bundle being dropped and opened the door.

How odd this is, he thought. I have asked no one to bring me twigs. Certainly I can use them to heat my hut, but they do not belong to me. I'll carry them inside and see if I can find the proper owner.

As Yidel lifted the twigs, he heard a clatter and bent down. A little sack caught inside the twigs had fallen to the floor, spilling its contents of gold coins all about.

Now what will I do with all this money that does not belong to me? worried Yidel. I cannot keep it in my house until I find its owner. It might not be safe here.

So Yidel decided to bring it to the rabbi. He would know what to do with it.

Yidel brought the coins and his story to Rabbi Levi. Then he waited patiently for the rabbi to tell him what to do.

The rabbi smiled at him. "Yidel, you have always been an honest man, having faith that God would help you in your time of need. Well, God has helped you. This money and the twigs are yours. Go back to your house and give your wife the good news. Then go straight to the synagogue. Thank God for sending you this great gift."

And Yidel did exactly as the rabbi told him to do.

Not only was Yidel able to buy a horse with the coins to help him haul his clay, but he had enough left over to build a machine for shaping bricks and a furnace to fire them in. He made sure to hire poor people in his factory and to find ways to help others, as God had seen fit to help him.

20
The Ring

abbi Shmelke heard a knock on his door. When he opened it, he saw a poor, stooped beggar.

"Please, wait a second," Rabbi Shmelke said, "and I will give you something."

Rabbi Shmelke searched through his coat pockets and pants pockets but could not find any coins. Then he remembered. He had emptied his pockets the night before when that other beggar knocked.

But I cannot send this man away empty-handed, Rabbi Shmelke thought. He looked around the kitchen. A bright object by the sink caught his eye, a ring. He gave it to the beggar.

Only a few minutes later, Rabbi Shmelke's wife Minde came home from her shopping at the market. The rabbi told her about the beggar and the ring.

"Oh, no," said Minde. "That ring is very valuable! It has a real diamond in it. You'd better run and catch up with that beggar."

It didn't take Rabbi Shmelke long to find the poor, stooped beggar, who looked surprised and frightened to see the rabbi running toward him.

"My friend," the rabbi called. "Stop a minute. I have something to tell you. That ring I gave you. My wife just told me it's worth a lot of money. Just make sure you get a good price when you sell it!"

21
Two Keys

tsik was a *mohel*, one who performs the ritual circumcision of baby boys on the eighth day after their birth. Itsik was a good man in many ways. He kept the commandments regarding ritual cleanliness and *kashrut* to the letter and had a kind manner with those about him. He never charged a poor family for his services and never refused a request to perform a circumcision.

Yet Itsik was very possessive about his money. He piled all his gold and silver coins in a large wooden chest that he locked always. He kept the brass key close by him on a chain he wore around his neck.

One morning, a magnificent carriage drove up to Itsik's house. A finely dressed coachman stepped down.

"Are you the *mohel*?" he asked.

"Yes," said Itsik.

"Please, my master needs your services. Can you come now?"

"I can," answered Itsik and took what he needed with him.

Itsik traveled a greater distance than he expected in this fine coach. He no longer recognized the coutryside around him. Finally, in some unfamiliar woods, the carriage stopped.

Itsik looked up at the ornate mansion before him. Gables and turrets and strange carvings covered the building. Never had he seen such a place!

The coachman took Itsik to the door, where an elderly housekeeper greeted him.

"My master called for you," she said.

Itsik nodded. "You will take me to the baby?" he asked.

"Yes, the baby," the housekeeper repeated. "But first I am to show you to the dining room."

Itsik followed her down a long passageway. There was something he did not like about this house. It was too quiet, not like the houses filled with happy relatives and laughter and toasting that went with all his other calls to perform a circumcision.

Pausing before the doorway, the housekeeper turned to Itsik. "I believe you are a good man," she said. "And so I will warn you. My master is not like you or me. He is not really a man. If you wish to live, you must not accept any food or drink from him or any gifts."

Itsik shivered at her words. What a strange woman, he thought. What an odd house. But having no choice, he clutched the tools of his trade tighter and followed her into an enormous dining hall.

Tables were covered with fine linens, glassware, and china. Plates of fishes and rolls, butter and cheeses, fruits—dried and fresh and candied—lay before him. It was here that he met his host, who looked normal enough. He was a young and handsome man, with a glossy black moustache and beard.

He does need to get out in the sun, though, Itsik thought. His skin is so white.

Having no desire to linger, Itsik immediately asked the master of the house to lead him to the baby.

"Oh, no," responded his host. "First, you must eat and drink. All this food has been placed here in your honor."

Remembering the woman's warning, Itsik said, "Oh, I am not hungry." It was then that he realized he had left his house without eating any breakfast and really was hungry.

"Since you will not eat," continued his host, "please, step in here and choose a gift for your payment."

The young man led Itsik into a room full of objects made of silver—candlesticks, wine goblets, and piles and piles of coins. "Please, choose something."

Still remembering the warning, Itsik refused these gifts as well, though his gaze lingered on the piles of coins.

"Perhaps these will please you more," said his host and led Itsik into an adjoining room full of golden vases, candelabra, and necklaces of precious stones.

Again, even though it greatly pained him, Itsik

said, "No, thank you. Only please lead me to your son, that I may do the circumcision you brought me here to perform."

"Oh, as to that," said his host. "Yes, the reason we brought you here. Please, follow me again."

By now, Itsik felt so weak with hunger and fear that he was not sure he could perform the circumcision. But he must. He followed his host into a bare, whitewashed room, empty except for dozens and dozens of keys of all shapes and designs that hung on hooks along the walls. Absently, Itsik glanced at the keys, and then his heart practically stopped its beating. Without thinking, he reached for his own key about his neck. It was still there.

Yet one of those keys hanging on that bare white wall was an exact duplicate of his own.

The young man noticed Itsik's look of recognition. "Yes, Itsik, that key is exactly like the one around your neck," he said. "And now I must tell you that I have not brought you here to perform a circumcision, for there is no baby."

Itsik stared at his host, trembling. He knew for certain now that the housekeeper's words were true. He did not face an ordinary man. What did he face, then? Suddenly, Itsik's eyes grew wide, for he knew.

"You must wonder why I have a copy of your key," continued the young man who was not a man. "I will tell you the reason. It is because whenever anyone orders a chest with a key in which to keep his coins, two keys are made. One belongs to the keeper of the chest, the other is God's. If God's key is not used, we hang it on this wall.

"You see, a person's money is not really his but God's as well. If you keep putting money into your chest and never take it out to offer it to those in need, then you lock your soul along with your money inside your chest.

"We are giving you another chance, Itsik. Here, take God's key with you and free your soul."

Itsik, shaking, took the key the angel of death offered him. Grateful for his second chance, he never again hoarded his money but gave freely to those in need. And never again did he look at that chest as his own, for he knew it was God's too.

22
Being Choosy

wealthy merchant lived in the very same town as Rabbi Zusya. He saw how poor the rabbi was, so each day he put some coins in the bag where the rabbi kept his *tefillin*, his leather prayer boxes.

The merchant did this day after day for many weeks and noticed that he grew richer. The more money he gave Rabbi Zusya, the more he had. And the more he had, the more he gave the rabbi.

Now this merchant knew that Rabbi Zusya was a student of the great Maggid of Mezritch, and so he shrewdly thought, When I give to Rabbi Zusya, my wealth increases. How much more will it increase if I give to the great Maggid!

The merchant began to travel regularly to Mezritch to give money to the great Maggid. But instead of growing wealthier, the merchant's fortune decreased.

Bewildered, the merchant went to Rabbi Zusya to ask him the reason. He told Rabbi Zusya the whole story.

"As long as you gave but did not care to whom, whether it was to me or some other, God gave to you and did not care who you were," answered the rabbi. "But when you decided to give your gifts to an especially important and distinguished person, God did likewise."

23
A Partner You Can Trust

eir the innkeeper was a mystery. Here was an ordinary man. True, he was an honest one, but he was no scholar of Torah, no teacher, no rebbe. Yet Meir was famous for miles around and people flocked to him. It was simple —his blessings worked miracles.

Rabbi Avraham of Apta, the Apta Rebbe, heard of Meir and wondered why God had given such an unusual gift to this humble innkeeper. He decided to go see Meir for himself and observe his ways. So he would not be recognized, Rabbi Avraham traveled alone and in a porter's clothes.

For three days, Rabbi Avraham rented a room at the inn and watched the innkeeper go about his business. Meir woke early. He said his morning prayers. He worked at his inn until nightfall. All these things every good Jewish innkeeper did.

And every day many people, old and crippled, young and sick, middle-aged and childless, came to

Meir for his blessings. Meir never tired but listened to each one and gave them a blessing. His blessings bore fruit.

There was only one little detail that caught Rabbi Avraham's eye—one unusual, tiny detail. Every time Meir took money from a customer, whether for a meal or a room at the inn, or for the care and feeding of horses, Meir would put half the coins in one cash box and the other half into a second one, identical to the first. Rabbi Avraham never saw what he did with the cash from the two cash boxes.

Since Rabbi Avraham could find no reason for the two boxes, on the fourth day, he approached the innkeeper. "I am Rabbi Avraham of Apta," he explained, "and I came here disguised as a porter to discover why you have been given this unusual gift of blessing. But I have seen nothing out of the ordinary in your behavior, except that you divide all your monies in half, half for one cash box and half for another."

Meir was flustered. Imagine, the famous Apta Rebbe was before him, asking him a question!

He lowered his head and answered. "I don't know myself why the Holy One has favored me with this gift. I am certainly no scholar or teacher or rebbe. But I can tell you about the two cash boxes. And perhaps such an honored rabbi as you will find some meaning in my story.

"I have always been a man of faith," began the innkeeper. "I've always trusted in God in good times and in bad.

"But once, our circumstances became so strained and business so poor that my wife would not leave me alone about her notion of getting a partner. She was convinced that with a partner's investment, we could turn around our terrible circumstances.

"But me? I feared taking on a partner. A partner can rob you, argue with you, order you about.

"Yet things got no better. The children were hungry and ill-clothed, and my wife saw no hope except in this idea of hers.

"So one day, I said I would go to town and look for a partner. Forgive me, Rabbi, but instead I went into the woods, where it is quiet.

"'God,' I said, 'What am I to do? I have always trusted You, and things have always worked out for us. But now look how things are. Am I to take a partner into my business? A total stranger? I would much rather have You as my Partner. You've always made a fine Partner. I promise to share all my profits with You. I hope it's a deal with You, because it's a deal with me.'

"I felt so good after my talk with God that I knew everything would be all right. I rushed home and told my wife I had found just the right Partner, one I could really trust. Then I started cleaning the inn with my newfound energy.

"Surprise! I'm dusting and straightening and come across a silver coin. Now I knew the partnership had really begun.

"With that coin I bought a second cash box and some wine for the inn. When I returned, I put the two cash boxes side by side on the counter. That way I wouldn't make a mistake and forget to give my Partner half the earnings.

"Ever since then, Rabbi, I have always divided my earnings in half and put my Partner's share in this box and mine in the other. At the end of each day, I take my Partner's share out of the box and give it away—to all the beggars who come to my inn and to the needy families in the village.

"Since I took on my Partner, my inn has prospered. My family has plenty of food and warm clothing, and my wife is happy.

"Do you think, Rabbi, that any of this helps you with your question?"

Rabbi Avraham smiled on the not-so-ordinary innkeeper. "Yes," he said. "Without a doubt. May you and your Partner continue to prosper." And the rebbe, dressed as a porter, left the inn, for the mystery was solved.

24
The Evil Urge

veryone in Berditchev knew Berish the miser. And everyone knew there was no use in asking him to donate to anything—to the widow, or the orphan, or the scholar. As a matter of fact, if a brave soul did venture forth to ask Berish for a contribution, he always met with the same response. Berish would take a rusty old coin from his pocket as his offering.

"But Berish," the brave soul would say, "surely you can give more."

"No, you'll not get any more from me than this," Berish answered. Then he would thrust his miserable coin back into his pocket, for it was always refused by the disgusted collector.

One day, the famous Rabbi Shneur Zalman came to Berditchev. He was collecting funds for the ransom of Jewish captives held by the authorities. These were usually poor people who owed money and could not repay their debts to the Polish landlords.

Rabbi Shneur Zalman was ready to knock on the door of every house in the city, but he was warned not to even try at a certain fine and substantial house belonging to Berish the miser.

When the rabbi and the local dignitaries walked by Berish's house, however, the rabbi insisted on knocking on the miser's door.

"Why allow yourself to be humiliated by this man?" Yonah, the town's mayor, asked.

"Like all of us, Berish is obligated to fulfill the *mitzvah* of *tzedakah*," said the rabbi. And he knocked.

Berish looked surprised to see such a distinguished group at his door. They must have the wrong house, he thought. Nevertheless, he invited them inside.

Rabbi Shneur Zalman began speaking immediately. "We have come to collect for the ransom of captives."

Berish reached into his pocket. The others hoped that just this once, Berish would not embarrass them all, and himself too, in front of this great *tzaddik*.

But as usual, Berish withdrew only the one rusty coin from his pocket and offered it to the rabbi. "This is my contribution. If you wish, take it. If not, I'll just put it back in my pocket."

The mayor and the other dignitaries were sure the rabbi would refuse the coin, as every other collector had. To their amazement, however, he accepted it and said calmly to his bookkeeper, "Please record Berish's gift."

The others got up to leave, but Berish stayed seated, motionless. Tears flowed from his eyes.

His visitors stopped and stared, transfixed. Something was the matter with Berish. They waited until finally Berish spoke. "Please, don't leave, Rabbi. I know I have not treated you as I should. Sit down again. I want *all* of you to stay and eat and drink with me."

Quickly, Berish covered the table with a fine white tablecloth, plates of nuts and cakes, glasses of tea and wine.

Now it was his guests' turn to sit motionless, dumbfounded, except for the rabbi. He smiled and said the blessings over the food.

"Eat! Drink, my friends!" shouted a now animated Berish. "It is not every day I am so honored to have a *tzaddik* like Rabbi Shneur Zalman and all the dignitaries of the city at my table!"

Overcoming their astonishment, his guests finally did eat and drink at Berish's table. They said a toast, a *L'Haim*, to Berish in honor of his sudden, unexpected hospitality, his amazing turnaround.

There was another toast, and another. Soon they were all clapping and singing and dancing too. People walking by Berish's house stopped to listen. Had Berish the miser's house been sold? they wondered. Had someone new moved in and no one told them?

No, that was surely Berish himself who put his head out the window to invite them in. Soon his spacious dining room was filled with half of Berditchev.

And then the rabbi started a *niggun*, a wordless tune, that quieted the crowd. "I want to say a few words on behalf of our host, Berish," the rabbi said when they finished singing the *niggun*. "We have all learned an important lesson today. Always we battle with our *yetzer hara*, our evil urge. Is this not so? What a bothersome thing this *yetzer hara* is, telling us to do what we know we shouldn't, trying to deprive us of our proper place in this world, trying to take from us our share in the World to Come. And, just to trick us, this evil urge assumes such different forms in each one of us.

"Poor Berish here! His *yetzer hara* had the best of him for years, telling him not to give *tzedakah*. That rusty copper coin stood in his way and never left his possession. Not even once did it allow him to give *tzedakah*.

"Finally, someone took his old coin, and now his heart is open. Since one *mitzvah* gives birth to another, our friend Berish is open to a whole new way, the way of *yetzer hatov*, the urge to do good."

Berish, his face glowing with a warmth beyond that of the hot tea and wine, thanked the rabbi. And, in front of all his guests, he said, "Please, Rabbi, call your bookkeeper. I have more to give your captives than that rusty old coin."

Glossary

Beit Hamidrash   A house of study, discussion, and prayer.

Etrog   Citron; a sweet-smelling fruit grown in Israel that resembles a lemon and is used during the holiday of Sukkot.

Gemara   The later rabbinic material that is part of the Talmud and is commentary on the *Mishnah*. It was compiled by the fifth century C.E.

Hallah   A loaf of bread, often baked in the form of a braid or twist, eaten on the Sabbath and on various Jewish festival days.

Hasid   (pl. *hasidim*)Disciple of a rebbe.

Heder   The Hebrew for room. Refers to an elementary-school classroom for the teaching of Judaism. A term most often used in Eastern Europe or among Jewish immigrants to other countries.

Kaddish   A prayer that praises God. It is used to separate parts of the prayer service and as a memorial prayer for the departed.

Kashrut   Pertaining to foods and eating utensils that are ritually permitted according to Jewish law.

L'Haim   Hebrew for "To life." Often used as a drinking toast, meaning "Here's to life."

Lulav   Palm branch. Bound with the myrtle and willow, it is used during the holiday of Sukkot with the *etrog.*

Maggid   A traveling preacher who teaches Torah through the telling of stories.

Midrash   Refers to the posttalmudic body of writings. In broad terms, *midrash* has come to mean a Jewish story that explains or clarifies an event or passage in the Torah. The word *midrash* comes from the root *derash*, which means "to search out."

Minyan   The required ten adult Jews needed to recite certain prayers and to perform certain ceremonies. (In an Orthodox service, the *minyan* must be made up of ten adult Jewish males.)

Mishnah   The earliest part of the Talmud, compiled by Rabbi Judah ha-Nasi about 200 C.E. It contains the Oral Law transmitted through the generations.

Mitzvah   (pl. *mitzvot*) Commandment from God. One of the 613 commandments in the Torah. The term is also used to mean a good deed.

Mohel   One who ritually circumcises a baby boy, usually on the eighth day after birth.

Niggun   A traditional tune or melody sung without words, especially among the *Hasidim.*

Passover   The eight-day festival commemorating the Exodus from Egypt and freedom from slavery. It is also called the Festival of Unleavened Bread or the Spring Festival.

Pasuk   A verse in the Bible.

Rabbi   A title meaning "my master." After the Middle Ages, the word *rabbi* came to mean a teacher, preacher, and the spiritual head of a Jewish congregation, as well as an interpreter and decider of the law.

Reb   A respectful form of address meaning "Mister." Used in Eastern Europe.

Rebbe   A hasidic master; leader of a hasidic community. Hasidism was a religious movement founded in Eastern Europe in the eighteenth century by the Baal Shem Tov, Rabbi Israel ben Eliezer.

Rosh Hashanah   A fall holiday, also called the Jewish New Year.

Ruble   A monetary unit used in Russia. In 1863, a tailor in Russia would earn no more than 120 rubles in a year.

Sabbath   Commemorates the seventh day, when God rested after creating the world. Jews also rest on this day and abstain from work, enjoying a day of spiritual refreshment.

Shavuot   A spring harvest holiday that celebrates the giving of the Torah on Mount Sinai.

Sukkot   Fall holiday commemorating the Israelites' forty-year journey through the desert after the Exodus from Egypt. Also called the Festival of Booths or Tabernacles.

Synagogue   A Jewish house of worship, assembly, and study.

Talmud   The most sacred Jewish text after the Bible, compiled from 200 B.C.E. to 500 C.E. A vast collection of rabbinic law, stories, thought, and commentaries on the Bible.

Tefillin   Phylacteries; two black leather boxes containing passages from Exodus and Deuteronomy. They are bound by black strips on the left hand and on the head and are worn for morning services on all days of the year except Sabbaths and scriptural holy days.

Torah   Teaching. Often refers specifically to the Five Books of Moses as distinct from the rest of the Bible, which includes the Prophets and Writings. In a broader sense, Torah refers to the whole of the Bible and the Oral Law.

Tzaddik   An especially righteous person.

Tzedakah Justice; righteous action toward those in need; sometimes has the meaning of charity.

World to Come Refers to the heavenly realm where righteous souls go after departing the earthly world, after death. Also called Paradise.

Yahrzeit The anniversary of a death.

Yeshivah School of higher Jewish learning.

Yetzer Hara The evil urge or evil inclination.

Yetzer Hatov The inclination for good.

Bibliography

Ausubel, Nathan. *A Treasury of Jewish Folklore*. New York: Crown Publishers, 1965.

Bin Gorion, Micha Joseph. *Mimekor Yisrael: Classical Jewish Folktales*. 3 vols. Bloomington, Indiana: Indiana University Press, 1976.

Buber, Martin. *Tales of the Hasidim*. New York: Schocken Books, 1991.

Certner, Simon (collected by). *101 Jewish Stories*. New York: Board of Jewish Education of Greater New York, 1987.

Citron, Sterna. *Why the Baal Shem Tov Laughed*. Northvale, NJ: Jason Aronson Inc., 1993.

Frankel, Ellen. *The Classic Tales*. Northvale, NJ: Jason Aronson Inc., 1989.

Ginzberg, Louis. *The Legends of the Jews*. 7 vols. Philadelphia: Jewish Publication Society, 1966-1968.

Goodman, Philip. *The Sukkot and Simhat Torah Anthology*. Philadelphia: Jewish Publication Society, 1973.

Gottlieb, Rabbi Naftoli. *My Brother's Keeper*. 2 vols. Trans. Uri Kaploun. New York: CIS Publishers, 1989.

Grishaver, Joel Lurie, and Huppin, Beth. *Tzedakah, Gemilut Chasadim and Ahavah*. Denver: Alternatives in Religious Education Inc., 1983.

Israel Folktale Archives (IFA), University of Haifa, Mount Carmel, Haifa 31999, Israel.

Klapholtz, Yisroel Yaakov. *Tales of the Baal Shem Tov*. Vol. 4. Trans. Sheindel Weinbach. Bnei Brak, Israel: Yisroel Klapholtz, 1980.

Mintz, Jerome R. *Legends of the Hasidim*. Northvale, NJ: Jason Aronson Inc., 1995.

Newman, Louis I. *The Hasidic Anthology*. Northvale, NJ: Jason Aronson Inc., 1987.

Noy, Dov. *Folktales of Israel*. Trans. Gene Baharov. Chicago: University of Chicago Press, 1963.

Pascheles, Wolff. *Jewish Legends of the Middle Ages*. Trans. Claud Field. London: Shapiro Valentine & Co., 1976.

Patai, Raphael. *Gates to the Old City*. Northvale, NJ: Jason Aronson Inc., 1988.

Prose, Francine. *Stories From Our Living Past*. New York: Behrman House, Inc., 1974.

Rabinowich, Jan. *The Tzedakah Workbook*. Rev. Jane Golub. Los Angeles: Torah Aura Productions, 1986.

Sadeh, Pinhas. *Jewish Folktales*. Trans. Hillel Halkin. New York: Anchor Books, 1989.

Scherman, Rabbi Nosson. *Tales From the Rebbe's Table.* Brooklyn, NY: Mesorah Publications, Ltd., 1986.

Siegel, Danny. *Gym Shoes and Irises: Personalized Tzedakah.* Spring Valley, NY: Town House Press, 1982.

Siegel, Danny. *Tzedakah: Jewish Giving, A Privilege.* New York: Tikum Olam Program of United Synagogue Youth, 1977.

ABOUT THE AUTHOR

Barbara Diamond Goldin currently teaches language arts to middle school students at Heritage Academy in Longmeadow, Massachusetts. She is the author of eleven children's books, including *Night Lights: A Sukkot Story*; nonfiction such as *Bat Mitzvah: A Jewish Girl's Coming of Age*; historical fiction such as *Fire: The Beginnings of the Labor Movement*; and collections of stories, including *A Child's Book of Midrash: Fifty-two Jewish Stories from the Sages*. Her books have received such awards and recognition as the National Jewish Book Award (for *Just Enough Is Plenty: A Hanukkah Tale*); the Sydney Taylor Picture Book Award (for *Cakes and Miracles: A Purim Tale*); and the American Library Association Notable Book Award for 1995 (for *The Passover Journey: A Seder Companion*). She lives in western Massachusetts with her two children.